BUILD
WINNI

BCS, THE CHARTERED INSTITUTE FOR IT

BCS, The Chartered Institute for IT champions the global IT profession and the interests of individuals engaged in that profession for the benefit of all. We promote wider social and economic progress through the advancement of information technology, science and practice. We bring together industry, academics, practitioners and government to share knowledge, promote new thinking, inform the design of new curricula, shape public policy and inform the public.

Our vision is to be a world-class organisation for IT. Our 70,000 strong membership includes practitioners, businesses, academics and students in the UK and internationally. We deliver a range of professional development tools for practitioners and employees. A leading IT qualification body, we offer a range of widely recognised qualifications.

Further Information
BCS, The Chartered Institute for IT,
First Floor, Block D,
North Star House, North Star Avenue,
Swindon, SN2 1FA, United Kingdom.
T +44 (0) 1793 417 424
F +44 (0) 1793 417 444
www.bcs.org/contact

http://shop.bcs.org/

BUILDING A WINNING TEAM

Technical leadership capabilities

Brian Sutton and Robina Chatham

Published by BCS Learning & Development Ltd, a wholly owned subsidiary of BCS, The Chartered Institute for IT, First Floor, Block D, North Star House, North Star Avenue, Swindon, SN2 1FA, UK.
www.bcs.org

ISBN: 978-1-78017-389-4
PDF ISBN: 978-1-78017-368-9
ePUB ISBN: 978-1-78017-369-6
Kindle ISBN: 978-1-78017-370-2

Ebook available

British Cataloguing in Publication Data.
A CIP catalogue record for this book is available at the British Library.

BCS books are available at special quantity discounts to use as premiums and sale promotions, or for use in corporate training programmes. Please visit our 'Contact us' page at www.bcs.org/contact

Typeset by Lapiz Digital Services, Chennai, India.
Printed and bound by Henry Ling Limited, at the Dorset Press, Dorchester, DT1 1HD

CONTENTS

LIST OF FIGURES AND TABLES

AUTHORS' BIOGRAPHIES

Professor Brian Sutton has over 40 years' management and leadership experience. He has developed comprehensive information systems (IS) strategies, conducted large-scale re-engineering initiatives and led major organisational change. He regularly contributes articles to professional journals and speaks at major professional gatherings. He holds a Doctorate in Corporate Education, a Master's degree in Information Systems Management from the London School of Economics and has worked extensively in both the private and public sectors in Europe and the United States. He was formerly a Professor of Systems Management in the Information Resources Management College of the National Defence University in Washington DC. He is currently Professor of Learning Performance with the Institute for Work-based Learning at Middlesex University.

Dr Robina Chatham has over 35 years' experience in IT. She has held positions that range from IT project manager within the shipbuilding industry to European CIO for a leading merchant bank and lecturer at Cranfield School of Management. She is qualified as both a Mechanical Engineer and a Neuroscientist. Previous books include *Corporate Politics for IT Managers: How to get streetwise*, *Changing the IT Leader's Mindset: Time for revolution rather than evolution*, and *The Art of IT Management: Practical tools and techniques*. Robina now runs her own company specialising in management development and executive coaching. She is also a visiting fellow at Cranfield School of Management and a research associate for the Leading Edge Forum. Her prime focus is on helping senior IT managers to increase their personal impact and influence at board level.

FOREWORD

I am unusual for a person of my age in that I have never learned to drive a car. I haven't got a licence. (It's a long story.) I recently decided that I wanted to learn about modern computer programming, which I hadn't done in anger for about 20 years. I picked up a book about the Python language, and began working my way through it. (Don't ask how far I got before I got distracted.) But, for both driving and programming in Python, I know what the skill is, I understand its scope, I knew I didn't know it, and I knew what it took to learn it, and how to learn it.

Leadership, and leading teams in particular, is a much more slippery thing. People are usually a bit unsure what it entails and what the exact scope of it is. They might kind of think they know how to do it. And they might confuse it with other skills, like project management, or just having good interpersonal skills.

Unfortunately, that just isn't good enough. You can have all the flashy technology, processes, projects and even talented people in the world. If you can't lead the people, and can't get them to work effectively, efficiently and happily in teams, the value won't come, for the company, the team or the individuals. Conversely, if you get the team leadership part right, all other good things follow: productive work, good choices, positive work environment, reputations, profits, sustainability.

The rub is that leadership isn't an area where we can benefit too much from just reading the theory. We need practical advice, grounded in real experience that we can experiment with. What Brian and Robina have done here is written a very concise, structured, pragmatic guide to leading teams. The simple, repeated structure of this book ensures that there are real world examples, exercises and questions, and further resource links for each of the areas covered. I believe this will be a very handy guide to those new to team leadership, and a nice reminder for those in the thick of it.

I have known Robina for 10 years, and am just getting to know Brian. It is no surprise to me that they have pulled off this feat. Well done to both.

To the reader, I wish you a fun and successful experience leading teams.

Dave Aron
Global Research Director, Leading Edge Forum

ACKNOWLEDGEMENTS

We would like to offer our sincere thanks to all the people who have attended our training courses around the world. You have inspired and motivated us to produce this work; the shape and content of this book came about as a direct result of your questions. So, when we sat down to write this book, we did not ask ourselves 'What do we know that we wish to tell other people?' Instead, we have built this book around your questions and the answers that you inspired in us, as we struggled to find the best ways of guiding you in your unique challenges. Without you, this book would never have seen the light of day.

To those of you who are familiar with our work, we hope that you will find renewed value in hearing again the ideas that we tried so hard to convey as we answered your questions. To those who are coming to us for the first time, we hope that some of the content will inspire you to see and be different and to find new understanding in your working relationships.

Last, but by no means least, we need to say a huge thank you to our respective partners, Angela and John. They are a constant support, and without their patience and understanding we could never have completed this book.

PREFACE

ACKNOWLEDGEMENTS

Most people who find themselves in a leadership position for the first time are lost and unprepared. The challenge of stepping up to leadership is not something that can be overcome by attending a course or reading a book that abstractly talks about planning or motivation or delegation. There is a big difference between understanding the theory of how something works and being able to apply those ideas in practice, especially if things are going wrong and you are under pressure to get results.

We work extensively with mid- and senior-level leaders in the IT sector across national boundaries and cultures. We find common issues whether we are working with technical team leaders or the senior leadership team – they all ask us similar questions and they always start with the words 'How do I...?'

But we have come to realise that generally they are not asking for theory; they already have the knowledge of what to do, they just have no idea of how to go about doing it in their particular situation and circumstances.

When you engage with someone as their leader, you are not simply directing work; you are engaged in creating and sustaining an environment within which those people can deploy their various talents to collectively achieve great outcomes – outcomes that make a real difference in the lives of business partners, clients, customers and constituents.

Successful leaders realise that success comes more through their ability to create and sustain positive emotional spaces for their people than from implementing best-practice processes.

Every situation that you face as a leader will have an element of uniqueness; every interaction will be coloured by the hopes, fears and aspirations of all parties. What makes leadership so difficult is that all too often you are unaware of your own driving forces, let alone those that drive the people you are leading.

When we are consulting with IT leaders at all levels we hear the same complaints – too much work, too few resources, too much change, conflicting priorities and customers who don't understand our problems. We see good people running faster just to stay in the same place and too many people facing 'burn out'. It need not be like this but it takes courage and focus from the leader to change the situation for everyone's benefit. In this book we look at five areas of focus that we have come to believe are critical to building and sustaining a winning team, getting the best out of yourself and everyone who works for you. The first thing to realise is that no leader can make a difference alone. To make a difference you need your team to follow your lead, to willingly commit their time, effort and talents to achieve great outcomes for your business partners.

In Chapter 1 we explore why someone would want to follow you. One reason they follow is because you, by virtue of your position, can bring them things; this may be tangible things such as resources or it could be more psychological support such as recognition. Either way you are best placed to help them if you are well connected and well respected in the wider organisational context. As such, Chapter 2 deals with building your circle of organisational influence. Sometimes your team will be engaged in routine tasks which are familiar, on other occasions they will be taking on new challenges in complex or politically charged situations; either way you need to get the right person with the right aptitude and attitude on the right task at the right time. Chapter 3 therefore looks at how to delegate for maximum impact. For a variety of reasons people don't always perform to expectations or to their own best ability; a leader cannot ignore these lapses and hope they get better on their own. In Chapter 4 we address the issue of dealing with poor performance. We are all under pressure to produce more with less. The answer is not to work longer hours, skip meals and run everywhere; what is required is focus. You need laser-like focus on your own activities and a similar approach to the activities of your team members. Focus on doing what matters to achieve the agreed outcomes and get rid of activities that eat time without contributing to results. We call this state behaving with a true sense of urgency and this is the focus of our final chapter.

Each of the chapters follows the same structure. Each chapter contains short anecdotes of how real people have applied some of the ideas in this book. We point to resources for you to develop a deeper engagement and understanding and we provide a series of simple things you can do now to start to develop into a more successful team leader.

Throughout the book you will see icons in the margin to focus your attention to particular aspects. Below you will find the key.

GOLDEN RULE

The golden rule to remember, even if you don't remember anything else about the chapter.

ANECDOTE

An anecdote or case study; real-life experience from leaders who have faced these situations and taken purposeful action

KEY IDEA

Key ideas to unlock potential. Things you should be trying to build into your professional practice

QUESTIONS TO ASK YOURSELF

Get into the habit of asking yourself these questions before you take action.

EXERCISE REGIMES

Things you can try immediately together with hints on how to adopt and adapt the ideas to your unique situation

RESOURCES

Links to resources where you can find additional helpful and inspiring ideas

We are always fascinated to hear of your experiences in applying the ideas we have presented. Please email us with examples from your personal experience and we will seek to include them in future editions of this book series.

Brian Sutton and Robina Chatham

drbriansutton@gmail.com
robina@chatham.uk.com

1 HELPING YOUR TEAM TO SEE YOUR VALUE TO THEM AS A LEADER

The focus of this chapter is helping your team to see your value to them as a leader. This involves learning to listen more than speak, to ask rather than tell, to open doors so people can shine, becoming attuned to the unusual or unexpected and above all making sure credit for good things always lands in the right place.

WHY IS THIS IMPORTANT?

Many IT people get promoted to a leadership position because they are good at their current job and that job is likely to be a technical one. The role of a leader is, however, very different from that of a 'doer'. Often IT people are expected to perform as a leader with little training, guidance or preparation and just to make this even more difficult, there are seldom good role models to follow. Sometimes you may find yourselves having to lead former 'workmates' and, other times, you may find yourself leading very intelligent technicians with little respect, or regard, for the leadership role. As you become a more experienced leader, you also become more distant from your technical roots and soon find that the people in your team know much more than you do about the technical aspects of their job. Whatever your circumstances, you need to earn the respect of your team.

Leadership is an art, rather than a science; it is not just about process and procedure: it is about communication, influence, teamwork and the ability to inspire and motivate others. It is about keeping your eyes open and your hands off, rather than your eyes down and your hands on. It is about asking the right questions, rather than searching for or providing the right answers.

THE IMPACT OF THE ISSUE

If your staff don't respect you or your role as their leader, you will not get the best out of them and sometimes you will get the very worst due to boredom, frustration or simply because 'they can't be bothered'.

If you are ineffective in your leadership role the organisation will have suffered a double whammy; it will have lost a valuable team member while gaining a poor leader. Principal reasons for this include:

- Poor communication – staff don't know what is expected of them or how they are meant to do it.
- Lack of teamwork – staff expend effort in 'doing their own thing'; there are no guiding principles to bring the individual members of the team together.
- Lack of a shared and compelling vision – there isn't anything for the team members to believe in; no group purpose or vision to see where they are heading.
- Lack of urgency – there is no drive, energy or motivation to perform and achieve.

MAKING SENSE OF IT ALL

Leadership is not about having all the answers or always being right; in fact one of the best ways of gaining trust from your team is to openly demonstrate some humility. Increasingly this is being termed 'Humble Leadership' and is characterised by a willingness to admit mistakes, empower followers and take risks for the greater good (that includes putting the needs of your organisation or team before your own needs).

Remember your success rests on the willingness of your team to volunteer their energy and initiative to your cause. Telling them what to do may produce short-term compliant behaviour but gaining their trust and releasing their potential is the only sure way of producing long-term commitment and results.

Your first duty should always be the welfare and growth of the people in your care. You should aim to create a climate in which others can shine.

HELPING A TEAM MEMBER

A new project manager saw an opportunity to support one of his team members. Bill was a brilliant technician with great ideas but was highly introverted and sought the background rather than the foreground. This lack of visibility meant that nobody outside the team knew how good he was. Bill's project manager helped him create a 'personal brand' highlighting his values, the reason to believe in him, the benefits of working with him and what made him unique. He also worked to help Bill see how his knowledge and insight related and contributed to wider issues within the business. As Bill started to engage more openly in the team his project manager worked to give him the opportunity to 'live his brand', first by sharing his ideas within the team and, as his confidence grew, by inviting him to a number of meetings with business partners, not as the tame 'techy expert' but as a valued colleague who could add an extra dimension to understanding and solving key issues. This increased Bill's visibility without ever stretching his comfort level too far. As wider exposure grew so did Bill's self-confidence. Six months later Bill received a well-deserved promotion.

As the leader, you enjoy levels of organisational access that are not available to your team. You get to hear things that they don't, you are invited into discussions that are closed to

3

them and your level of organisational autonomy allows you to access resources and leverage relationships that can help your teams work with much less stress. Your team has to play the hand of cards that it is dealt, but your position allows you the opportunity to stack the deck slightly in its favour.

Learn to exercise your position and influence for the benefit of your team. Ensure your team members take the credit for their achievements and get the exposure that they deserve.

BRINGING DEVELOPMENT AND OPERATIONS TOGETHER

A new team leader told the story of how animosity between Development and Operations was getting in the way of his teams' project implementations. He adopted the role of mediator or 'marriage counsellor', bringing the two sides together. The team leader facilitated a discussion whereby the Development manager agreed to follow the process as laid down by Operations willingly in exchange for a commitment from Operations to introduce a new 'fast track' process for urgent changes. Both parties were pleased with the outcome and general relations and results improved significantly.

PRACTICAL ADVICE

Successful team leadership requires you to simultaneously operate at multiple levels of both attention and abstraction. You need to be able to focus on important details whilst never losing sight of the greater goal; this ability to zoom in and zoom out is a key skill and not a simple one to master. You also need to exercise your influence and relationship-building skills in every direction: downwards, sideways and upwards.

QUICK WINS

A new IT manager identified the 10 key influencers and adversaries of IT. She then engaged in a relationship-building exercise whilst at the same time gathering information about pain points, irritating niggles and what was keeping the team awake at nights. Armed with this intelligence she identified a number of quick wins. This won her much credibility and demonstrated the value of her leadership role; it cemented relationships within the team and with the wider organisation that came to value and view IT in a different light.

Increasingly as you move to more senior positions, technical ability counts for less than your relational skills; it becomes less about knowing 'stuff' and more about a way of seeing differently, communicating widely and wisely and evoking a passion within your listeners. Ultimately you need to find a new way of being in the world.

As a personal health check, which of the behaviours listed in Table 1.1 best describe your current leadership behaviours?

Table 1.1 Dos and don'ts of team leadership

Do	Don't
• Value your staff and take an interest in them personally.	• Try to be one of the lads, but neither should you distance yourself.
• Demonstrate, through action, that you can do things for them that they could never hope to achieve without you.	• Do their jobs for them, micro-manage them or abdicate responsibility.

(Continued)

5

Table 1.1 (Continued)

Do	Don't
• Ensure they have the tools, resources and necessary access to training to do the things they commit to.	• Shut them out or overtly take credit for their successes.
• Give the credit to your team and open doors for them to demonstrate their capability in more senior circles.	• Expect your staff to read your mind.
	• Be too prescriptive about how to achieve a certain task.
• Leave room for creativity and innovation, and give them the opportunity to do it their way.	• Blame your team when things go wrong – you can delegate authority, but not accountability.
• Monitor their progress, coach and develop them and give them feedback.	• Say one thing, but do another.
	• Lie to them – you will be found out and it will destroy trust.
• Nurture and reward talent, and involve them in selecting and growing new talent.	• Play one team member off against another.
• Build mutual trust through supportive actions.	• Look for opportunities to criticise.
• Be open and honest.	
• Look for opportunities to praise.	

THINGS FOR YOU TO WORK ON NOW

Below are some questions to help you diagnose where you are now and what aspects of your professional persona as a team leader are most in need of development. Think carefully about these questions and regularly build in time to reflect honestly upon how you are performing against these criteria.

?

KEY QUESTIONS TO ASK YOURSELF

- How do my staff view my role as their leader? What do they think I spend my time doing? Do they feel I justify my salary?

- What do my team think of me personally? What do they say about me when I am not in earshot? Do they feel they can talk to me about their problems or ask for help when they need to?

- Do I genuinely care about my team? What do I do to encourage and develop them?

- What behaviours earn me respect? What more could I do?

- What behaviours earn me trust? What more could I do?

- Do I show favouritism or do I treat everyone equally?

- Do I unconsciously recruit in my own likeness or do I genuinely value diversity in all its forms?

- Does every member of my team feel that they have grown in the past year? If so, what can they do now that they could not do a year ago, and what specific action of mine was the key enabler of that growth?

Reflect on your answers and build yourself a prioritised action plan to make progress on your top three areas of concern. Give yourself tangible and measurable goals.

Below are some simple practical steps that you can start to build into your routine. If some of this is alien to your natural character and demeanour you may want to build up slowly. Just be sincere and be consistent.

MINI EXERCISES YOU CAN TRY IMMEDIATELY

- Do the rounds every morning for a month and see the difference. Ask how your team is getting on; take an interest in their work and them as individuals. Take a note of key people and events in their lives. Ask questions like 'How did Andrea get on with her A levels?', and so on.

- Listen twice as much as you speak. Show that you value what you have heard. Look for opportunities to build upon ideas that come from your team and then make sure that you publicly attribute the source of the idea if it proves successful.

- Engage privately and thoughtfully with each member of your team and ask them what more you could do to help them deliver in their roles. Take simple actions that liberate their talent and develop their skills.

- Make it very clear that mistakes are ok, indeed valuable when you are trying something new or innovative. Mistakes are not ok when you are doing routine tasks that are not complex and which you have done many times before.

- Be open about your own failings and say and do things that demonstrate your own commitment to learning new things from any source.

- Keep them informed – provide messages from on high, insights about the company, your industry sector and the market you operate in.

- Tell the truth and nothing but the truth, recognising, however, that you will sometimes need to be economical with the truth. If you can't tell them, be honest and tell them that you can't tell them.

- Always speak well of others in front of your team – that way they will think you will speak well of them (rather than badly) when they are not within earshot.

If you are inspired to find out more about any of the themes covered in this chapter we suggest that you start by reviewing the resources listed below.

FURTHER FOOD FOR THE CURIOUS

Chatham R. (2015) *The Art of IT Management: Practical tools, techniques and people skills.* Swindon: BCS:

- Combining simple models and powerful examples, this book is a must read for new and more seasoned IT managers alike.

Collins J. (2005) Level 5 Leadership: The triumph of humility and fierce resolve. *Harvard Business Review*, July–August. Available from https://hbr.org/2005/07/level-5-leadership-the-triumph-of-humility-and-fierce-resolve [21 March 2017]:

- An excellent insight into what makes a leader truly great – a paradoxical mixture of personal humility and professional will.

Prime J. and Salib E. (2014) The Best Leaders are Humble Leaders. *Harvard Business Review*, 12 May. Available from https://hbr.org/2014/05/the-best-leaders-are-humble-leaders [21 March 2017]:

- An interesting report of the findings of a wide-ranging international study that points to ways in which leaders can increase feelings of involvement and belonging in their teams.

Valcour M. (2016) How to Know Whether You're Giving Your Team Needless Work. *Harvard Business Review*, 26 August. Available from https://hbr.org/2016/08/how-to-know-whether-youre-giving-your-team-needless-work [21 March 2017]:

- This identifies the concept of 'illegitimate tasks' and shows how they arise and proliferate. Some good practical tips for how to keep these illegitimate tasks in proportion.

2 INCREASING YOUR CIRCLE OF ORGANISATIONAL INFLUENCE

The focus of this chapter is on developing relationships both within and external to your team and then leveraging those relationships for the benefit of all.

WHY IS THIS IMPORTANT?

People tend to do business with, and refer people to, people they know, like and trust. The more people there are who know and trust you, the more referrals you will get. This is obviously important if you are a small business owner or are in sales and marketing, but it is also equally important in every organisational setting. As an IT leader, you may wish to sell the benefits of a piece of new technology to a business partner; alternatively you may wish to give your board a wake-up call on the potential impact of digital disruption.

Cast your mind back to that excruciating experience at school when you all stood in a line while two sporting stars picked their teams. They did not necessarily pick the best players; they picked the people they knew, liked and trusted. If you were new and unknown, you were left until last and nobody wanted you.

It is just the same in organisations. The people who get the interdepartmental transfers, the special courses, the places on the cross-functional action teams, one of the very few places on the company awayday – these are the people who are known, trusted and respected far beyond their work team or department.

If you want to get on, you need to raise your visibility and start working on your sphere of influence.

Some would call this networking. Now, when we talk about networking, we are not talking about the use of social networking tools, such as Facebook or LinkedIn. While they are both fine tools and very useful, they lack the key element, the 'ingredient X' – a sense of how much you **trust** someone. You don't come to trust somebody by clicking on a web page; you can become inquisitive about someone, you can even develop the beginnings of a sense of liking, but trust can only be built through face-to-face interaction over a significant period of time.

When we talk of networking, we are talking about a purposeful social interaction that builds a trusting relationship and results in someone being willing to risk their own reputation by recommending you.

THE IMPACT OF THE ISSUE

In organisations, as in life, who you know, how they think about you and their willingness to put their reputation on the line to help you has a far bigger influence on what you can achieve than anything you can do on your own. Your circle of influence is key to your success – make it your business to build and expand it so that when you are faced with a daunting task, you look up for help and find that you are surrounded by willing hands who have your best interests at heart.

CREATE HUMAN MOMENTS

One of the authors was recently attending a conference for business relationship managers (BRMs) as a speaker. During her talk she asked the audience of over 75 BRMs how they spent their lunchtimes. Bearing in mind that their role is about building relationships across their respective organisations, over two-thirds admitted to spending their lunchtimes 'eating a sandwich whilst catching up on their email'.

It ought to be a no-brainer that someone with the title 'relationship manager' should direct their efforts to meeting people, building rapport and trust, and learning about the challenges that others are facing. But whatever your job title, if you are leading a team you need to make relationship building a key area of focus. You cannot achieve this sitting at your desk staring at a screen.

MAKING SENSE OF IT ALL

When some people talk of a circle of influence, they do so in an attempt to give you a focus for your attention. In his book *The 7 Habits of Highly Effective People*, Stephen R. Covey distinguishes between:

- **Our circle of concern** – all the things that might interest us on which we can focus our energy. Our circle of concern may be made up of things like our family, our mortgage, our job, the economy, global warming, heart disease, educational inequality, the state of the health service and so on. Although these may all be noble causes, some clearly lie outside our ability to have a direct influence.

- **Our inner circle of influence** – this is a smaller subset of the circle of concern and is made up only of those things that you can actually do something about.

Covey argues that by learning to focus on those things that you can do something about, that you have some control over, you can become more proactive, productive and energised. Wasting your time and energy worrying about things over which you really have no control is counter-productive. He goes further in suggesting that if you focus too much on the wider circle of concern, the things that you have no control over, the effect can be to increase feelings of negativity, which, in turn, can have the effect of reducing your circle of influence.

There is no doubt that where you focus your attention and energy is important, and there is considerable merit in the idea that you should prioritise those areas where your skills, knowledge, experience, and mental and emotional connection allow you to make the biggest difference. However, when we talk about circle of influence, we are talking about building relationships with people: how you can build deeper, more trust-based relationships, and techniques that you can use to dramatically increase the number of people that you know and who trust you.

Trust is the key word because people do business with, and refer people to, people they know, like and trust. It is as simple as that.

SPEAK THE SAME LANGUAGE

The chief information officer (CIO) of a bank was keen to implement DevOps (software development/information technology operations). He sent two members of his DevOps team to elicit the support of the banking director, a key stakeholder. After two hours of 'blinding him with science' the two technicians were sent away with 'fleas in their ears'. The CIO then had a rethink and asked for the help of a team leader. The team leader worked in a different area but was good at relationship management and had built a good relationship with the banking director. She met with the banking director and prepared one high-level, clever but simple slide that explained the concept of DevOps and the value it could bring to the business. She won the support of the banking director whilst also improving the reputation of the CIO.

But trust is such an ephemeral quality – how often do you see someone briefly in a TV programme and think, 'I wouldn't trust them'? Perhaps you look at someone in the street, or in a shop, and think 'I wouldn't trust them'. It is human nature to make initial assessments of trust on pretty tenuous information. Maybe this is because learning to trust someone takes time and effort. You risk having your trust abused and, if this happens, you become even more reluctant to make the effort again.

So, one of the key factors in your willingness to make the effort to trust someone may be your assessment of how useful you feel that person may be to you in the future. If you feel that they may be helpful, you are more inclined to make an effort to get to know them.

Once you start to engage with someone, you may find that they can indeed be helpful to you, in which case you are likely to invest even more time and effort to maintain your acquaintance. If they then go on to be helpful, you invest your trust in them and you feel an obligation to be helpful in return.

Put bluntly – trust is the way you measure someone's willingness to go out on a limb to help you.

If you make an effort to help someone get what they want, and you do it in an ethical and honest manner, you will increase their level of trust in you and, in return, you build a bond of obligation that you can call upon at a later date.

This leads us nicely to our central question, which is – **How can I create opportunities to interact with more people in a way that encourages them to like me and trust me?**

The obvious answer is that you need to network more. But before you rush off to meet more people, let's take a moment to understand what networking is:

- Networking **is** a purposeful human interaction with the sole aim of building trust. You do this by focusing on the other person, their needs and what you can do to help them fulfil their needs.

- Networking **is not** selling, either yourself or your product; it is certainly not an opportunity to boast of your achievements or prowess. It is not small talk, because that has no purpose or useful outcome other than passing time; nor is it an opportunity to practise amateur psychoanalysis or run a self-help clinic.

Networking as a means of marketing yourself is a skill that needs to be understood and practised. It is much more than just meeting people and, despite the hype of technology-enabled professional networking tools, it is also much more than just getting connected online.

KEEP YOUR PROMISES

A young and personable team leader working for a small software house was attending a conference. During the drinks reception at the end of the day she met a development manager of a Fortune 500 company. After a very interesting and amicable conversation she promised to send the development manager a white paper on a certain subject. She duly did. Two weeks later she received an email from the development manager thanking her for the paper and saying how useful it had been. She also received an invitation to present her own firm's products and services at the company's next IT leadership team meeting. After the presentation, the development manager said to the young team leader, 'It is so unusual in this day and age for someone to deliver on a casual promise such as you did, thank you!' Subsequently the software house received its biggest order ever from the Fortune 500 company.

In his 1999 article, 'The Human Moment at Work', Edward M. Hallowell set out the two conditions that must be simultaneously present for a human moment to happen: physical presence, and emotional and intellectual engagement.

The same is true for your networking efforts because, when you network, you are creating a human moment. However, in today's world, with remote working and virtual teams, physical presence is often a challenge. When physical presence is not an option there is no easy solution. Video-conferencing tools, such as Skype, are useful but not a substitute; the limits on sound frequency filter out tone and voice inflections. Body language is not the same; it is often contrived or static, there is a time lag and frequently quality issues, depending on your internet connection. Quite frequently these days, in business conversations, people choose to turn the video option off – they may be working from home and feel they are not dressed appropriately or want to be free to multi-task unseen. Our advice is:

- When you do have the chance to meet and talk to strangers face-to-face make the most of the opportunity; don't waste those precious moments by spending your time on your email communicating back home.

- When you are communicating remotely be very thoughtful in your use of tone – consider how your message may come across to the receiver: is there any ambiguity, could your message be misconstrued, how may someone from a different culture or background perceive your message? Also, try to engage in a little small talk and find that personal connection to create a lasting bond.

- If at all possible, try to ensure that your first meeting is face-to-face – it will be so much easier to find that personal connection to create that lasting bond. Also you will significantly reduce the chance of things going wrong.

As your purpose is to build liking and trust, it also follows that your focus should be firmly on the person you are engaged with, their needs and how you may fit into fulfilling those needs. By doing so, you can demonstrate your value to them by helping them to achieve their goals.

Set your own goals aside; there will be time enough to get around to those once you have built the trusting relationship.

PRACTICAL ADVICE

We have seen that if you want to increase your circle of influence, you have to get out there and network; that means you build relationships with everybody and anybody you come into contact with who could be of value to you in the future.

You may feel a little daunted by this prospect because you cannot assess people's potential value to you, unless you take the trouble to get to know them, and you don't have the time to get to know everyone you bump into. As such, you need to establish a strategy on how to target and prioritise your networking efforts.

We suggest that you work on the following groups in this order:

- Inside your organisation: make it your business to find out who the key players are in each department, who is sponsoring each major project or programme, who is managing each project on behalf of the sponsor and who reports directly to board members. These are all people who should be in your circle of influence – you need to make opportunities to interact with these people and find out what you can do for them, even if it is something as simple as introducing them to someone else. Make it your business to do something for them and show them they can rely upon you.

- Outside your organisation, but inside your professional discipline: you already have something in common – your area of expertise. Now look for a way to leverage that – you may be able to help them solve a problem, access a resource that is unknown to them or introduce them to like-minded people. This may be a longer-term pay-off, but it is time well spent. Look for opportunities to engage with people in communities, such as:
  - your customer community – the people who use and care about the goods and services that you provide;
  - specialist groups under the banner of your professional body;
  - journalists (both retained and freelance) who write on your subject;
  - conference organisers and speakers.
- Outside your professional discipline, but working in the same sector as you: this is playing the long game, but it does have two big advantages:
  - It helps you understand the needs and drivers of people who face different problems from you, and gives you valuable practice at building relationships where you don't have a common bond of professional knowledge.
  - It can give you new insights that you would never pick up by interacting with like-minded people – this sort of boundary spanning is a key skill and makes you a valued asset on cross-functional teams.

OK, so now you have narrowed down the universe to a manageable 15 to 25 people that you will target in order to expand your circle of influence.

In addition, make it your mission to give a little to the people you come across each day who are generally ignored by the masses, such as security guards, car-park attendants, cleaners, drivers, receptionists and so on. Acknowledge their existence, engage in a little small talk and look for an opportunity to compliment or thank them. People like to feel valued for who they are and what they do, and people in such professions are vital, but rarely noticed or acknowledged. They also have their own network and pretty soon word will get around – 'that one is OK', 'he's not stuck up like the rest', 'she made my day'. Remember that value can come out of the most unlikely acquaintanceships.

To do this you will have to be generous with yourself and your time because you never know what you might need from someone in the future. As they say, 'be nice to people on your way up because you might meet them on your way down'.

Now for some general advice on sensible tactics to follow when engaging with someone you want to influence. This is a long list, and we suggest that you start by choosing one or two ideas and building them into the way you do things. Once these have become embedded as good habits, revisit the list and choose two more areas to work on:

- Always speak well of others; never slag anyone off behind their back. If you say something bad about someone to someone else, how does that someone else know that you are not doing the same to them behind their back?

- Take an interest in other people and their activities and interests. For most people, their favourite topic is either themselves or the achievements of members of their family. Listen carefully; this is how you get to know someone and find out about their values and what is important to them.

- Develop the ability to converse on a wide range of subjects – your aim is to show that you know just enough about what they are saying to recognise that they are making a really valuable contribution and to be able to ask meaningful questions that give them the opportunity to impress you some more. Resist the temptation to show them how much you know on the topic.

- Look for common interests – these will always provide an easy, non-threatening ice-breaker on any occasion.

- Actively listen to others and accept that they have a valid point of view, even if you don't agree with it. If you can learn how they see the world and why they see it like they do, you will be better placed to assess how you can help each other.

- Praise, rather than criticise, and never, ever argue with someone. You cannot win an argument – if you lose, you have lost and if you win, you have lost because you have just created a grievance in the mind of the other person and potentially destroyed any chance of that person ever trusting you.

- Demonstrate empathy and sensitivity to the moods and feelings of others. You need to engage emotionally as well as intellectually.

- Respect and value people for who they are without trying to change them.

- Demonstrate modesty and humility and be prepared to admit your mistakes or that you are wrong. Develop your sense of humour and ability to laugh at yourself.

- Put yourself out to help others without expecting anything in return.

Finally, try to end every interaction with an enquiry that gets to the heart of how you can help them. This is your trump card because it demonstrates that you have been listening and that you care about them, and it gives you an opportunity to start another interaction with them at a later date. But you need to be a little subtle about how you do it.

Here are some ideas that you can adapt and adopt to your own situations:

- If you are building rapport with someone inside your business, but outside your discipline, try something like:

- ■ 'Wow, I had no idea what your programme was trying to achieve, it sounds really exciting. But from what you've said, your biggest issue seems to be that you are lacking a skilled "x" – can you tell me more about what you need from this person, so that I can keep my eyes out for someone who might fit the bill?'

- • If you are building your business and looking for prospects for yourself, don't ask outright; use reverse psychology, show you want to help them find prospects and you can be sure that when you do, they will return the favour. Try something like:

  - ■ 'How would I recognise someone who would be a good prospect for you?'

Notice with both the examples above that you are feeding back to them that you have intellectually engaged with their issue and you are on their emotional wavelength with regard to their immediate needs. Also, by asking them for a pen picture of what they need to solve their issues, you have left them with a lasting impression that you are actively engaged with them to solve their problem. Even if you don't actually help them this time, they will remember your interest and willingness to go out of your way for them. You have started to build trust and obligation.

THINGS FOR YOU TO WORK ON NOW

The focus of this chapter has been the importance of trust and building trust-based relationships. We have recommended a form of purposeful networking that requires you to first give generously of your time and resources; it involves listening attentively and giving openly.

Here are some questions to help you diagnose what you need to be working on.

KEY QUESTIONS TO ASK YOURSELF

- What do you hope to achieve in the next 12 months and who could help you achieve it?

- What have you done in the past two weeks to build a new relationship with someone in your organisation?

- Last time you went to a conference or professional gathering, how many new people did you get to know and how many of them did you subsequently help in any way?

- What are you currently doing to build professional links with people outside your organisation?

Reflect on your answers and use the simple practical tools listed below to help you build a prioritised action plan.

MINI EXERCISES YOU CAN TRY IMMEDIATELY

- Make a list of the 10 most influential people in your team; include the business partners or clients that they currently interact with. Plot them on a diagram, showing their relationships to senior leaders and to each other.

- Repeat the same diagramming exercise for the 10 most influential people in your department or business unit.

- Repeat the same diagramming exercise one last time focusing on who you believe to be the 10 most influential people you have met in your organisation. How many of these people know who you are, trust you and would ask for you if they were staffing up an important project?

- Look at the relationship maps that you created in the previous exercises. Prioritise three people from each map that you want to work on to build greater trust and understanding. Devise a strategy to make it happen and commit yourself to three actions that you will complete in the next 10 days.

Understand that although we advise you to do something now, building a relationship with people is not a 'one shot' activity. It takes time and multiple small but significant acts. Be yourself, don't rush in and try to force an entry. Listen carefully and when the opportunity arises act with simple, open sincerity in a spirit of helpfulness.

FURTHER FOOD FOR THE CURIOUS

Covey S.R. (2004) *The 7 Habits of Highly Effective People – Powerful lessons in personal change.* London: Simon & Schuster:

- Lots of useful self-improvement guidance based on identified winning habits; needs deep study to get the best out of it.

Hallowell E.M. (1999) The Human Moment at Work. *Harvard Business Review,* January–February. Available from https://hbr.org/1999/01/the-human-moment-at-work [21 March 2017]:

- A classic *Harvard Business Review* article that makes the social and psychological case for ensuring that you create the time and space to have meaningful human interaction and points to the potentially dire consequences when you don't make the effort.

Yemm G. (2008) Influencing Others – A key skill for all. *Management Services,* 52 (2). 21:

- A short, four-page article that introduces and expands on influencing strategies and tactics.

3   DELEGATING WORK FOR MAXIMUM IMPACT

The focus of this chapter is growing capability by delegating meaningful tasks and learning to let go.

WHY IS THIS IMPORTANT?

Hands up all of you who don't have enough to do. We guess that not many hands went up. In fact, most of you probably have far too much to do, feel stressed that you can't keep up with all the demands on your time and seldom leave the office at the appointed hour.

We believe that if you did an honest audit of how you spend your time, you would find that about a third is spent doing tasks that you really shouldn't be doing and about another third is spent in meetings where you make little or no contribution. All of this means that, on average, only about a third of your available time is spent doing meaningful things that might actually produce value for your organisation or develop the people under your care. Let's look in a little more detail at the first two categories.

So why do you spend time doing things that don't necessarily need to be done by you? There are a number of reasons. Maybe they are things you were good at before you got promoted and you feel that you do them best or perhaps you just like doing them. Alternatively, you may feel that you are the only person that will do the job 'right'. You could say that the time that you spend doing all of the above represents your **potential** energy, time that you could free up in order to do something more beneficial for your organisation.

Now let's look at the third of your time that you spend in meetings or dealing with organisational noise that has little or no relevance to your day job. This includes drafting long and complicated responses to emails on which you were just a 'cc' addressee, and attending meetings where you have no useful input but you feel that your organisational position demands that you are seen to be present, or just the fear of missing out (FOMO). Generally, we find that this sort of frantic organisational arm-waving depletes your time and energy, but usually fails to produce anything in the way of valuable organisational results. You could say that this represents your **kinetic** energy, energy that you could redirect towards more purposeful ends.

The chances are that you have considerable stores of untapped **potential** and **kinetic** energy. The scientists among you will know that you cannot create new energy, but you can certainly redirect the energy that you have. The good news is that the number-one way of redirecting your energy as a manager is the art of delegation.

THE IMPACT OF THE ISSUE

All leaders have a duty to develop their people, so that they can achieve their full potential and, in so doing, contribute to the broader business success. This element of the leader's role is a form of organisational stewardship that requires a level of selflessness and a willingness to see the key role of management as developing people. Alas, in our experience, we find that many leaders strike the wrong balance between task and people focus. It may be that they have had little exposure to people management skills in their education and have achieved their position as a result of excellent performance in their technical specialism. But, as a leader, your organisational value lies not in what you can do, but, rather, in what you can enable others to do; this is rooted in your ability to delegate.

Leaders who fail to delegate, or who delegate poorly, are failing their organisation and failing in a duty of care to their people. Failure to delegate appropriately will lead to:

- people not realising their talents and underperforming;
- people not knowing what they are supposed to be doing;
- people working at cross purposes or in general confusion;
- missed deadlines, increased stress and burn-out;
- a vacuum when you need to move on and no one has the skills to succeed you. Indeed, one of the biggest issues that organisations face at all levels of leadership is succession.

MAKING SENSE OF IT ALL

Delegation is about giving up part of your job with the two prime objectives of: growing the people who report to you; creating space in your own diary, so that your own boss can grow you by delegating part of their job to you.

If these are not your objectives, you will be effectively 'dumping' or 'offloading'; and just as you don't like to be dumped on, it is not nice to do it to others.

LET GO OF YOUR COMFORT BLANKET

Harry was a detailed person and had a tendency to micro-manage. He would not only delegate the 'what' and 'when' but also the 'how'. In addition, he failed to explain the 'why', that is, the context. As a consequence, his team never felt that they owned a task and had no opportunity to express their strengths or put their mark on their work. This was highly demotivating and demoralising.

Delegation is really important; you have to find a way to do it and make it work for you and your people. Understanding why managers avoid delegation is the first step towards developing your own coping strategies.

There are three principal psychological barriers to delegation:

- **It often involves giving up jobs that you like doing** – this is the difference between being efficient and being effective. You write code efficiently, but being effective is about directing your efforts to the right job.

- **It usually involves overcoming the fear of losing control** – people often think (sometimes rightly) that nobody else can do the job as well as they can. Therefore, when you give a task to someone, you then unfairly judge the quality of what they produce and often end up redoing all or part of it to your own exacting standards – this creates needless extra work and stress that could have been avoided.

- **There is a need to balance two, potentially competing, psychological contracts** – one with your own leadership or customer who wants the outcome of your delegated task, and one with the person you delegated to who is looking to you for help and development. These contracts tend to be implicit, rather than explicit, and leaders are often lax at making sure that everyone's expectations are aligned.

In addition to the psychological barriers, there is also the practical barrier that delegation takes time and effort. You need to select the right person, brief them properly, spend extra time guiding their efforts and reviewing their progress, and, finally, you need to check their output. This all takes time and, unless you create the time and space to do it properly, the chances are that your delegation process will just end in frustration and confusion.

ESTABLISH UNDERSTANDING BEFORE ACTING

Bert was a big picture person and when he delegated a task he would give a high-level instruction followed with a wave of the hand that signalled 'just get on with it'. When asked for more detail he would say, 'you understand, you can do it'. The problem was that his instructions were open to many interpretations. The consequences were that when one of Bert's team delivered on a task, if it did not meet Bert's expectations, Bert would say 'do it again' or 'try harder'. Eventually, and by a process of trial and error, his team would reach the desired outcome but with significant amounts of wasted time and effort and much demotivation and demoralisation.

When you delegate a task, you need to take full responsibility for ensuring that all parties have total clarity about what is expected and how the quality and usefulness of the output will be judged. But this is not a 'one size fits all' process. Each person has differing levels of ability, willingness and desire to engage and each person has differing levels of confidence and processes information in different ways. (See practical advice later in this chapter.)

Even when you manage to overcome the psychological and practical barriers that stop most leaders from delegating, you are still faced with the issue of organisational responsibility. You need to remember that you can delegate tasks and the authority to do those tasks, but you cannot delegate accountability. You are the leader; if it all goes wrong you are accountable because you have managed unwisely. Pointing downwards and claiming 'the dumb cluck let me down' is just another way of saying 'I'm a useless leader who doesn't know what I am doing and can't see what is happening around me'.

The buck stops with you; if you delegate and someone screws up, that someone is you.

DELEGATE TO GROW PEOPLE

A boss gave one of his junior managers the opportunity to present to the Board. The boss coached and supported the junior manager throughout the process; he also encouraged and boosted the confidence of his junior manager. The presentation was a great success and IT won the Board's approval for a multi-million pound project. The boss had demonstrated the courage and humility to delegate part of his job and also demonstrated confidence in his junior manager. Clearly, he had no fear of losing control.

So now let's look at some things that you can start to do now that will help you overcome all the barriers and become great at the art of delegation.

PRACTICAL ADVICE

When you come to delegate there are some golden rules that should guide you regardless of who you are dealing with or the nature of the task. You should always:

- Start with the outcome: paint a clear picture of what needs to be achieved and how success will be measured.

- Brief people fully: make sure that constraints and boundaries are explained and that they have access to the information needed.

- Wind backwards from the deadline: if the output is needed by close of business next Friday, you need to set a deadline of close of business Wednesday. Remember, they probably haven't done the task before, and so they will need more time and you will need time to check and possibly polish the output.

- Open any doors that need to be open, so that they have access to the people and resources that they will need. Remember, unless you inform others what is going on, they may not get timely access to people and information.

- Take your hands off, but keep your eyes open – be available for advice and check on key points (as appropriate).

Who you delegate to is just as important as how you delegate. You need to be careful that your chosen person has not only the skills and knowledge, but also the desire to take on the task. Not every task can, or should, be delegated and not everyone is ready to be delegated to. Figure 3.1 sets out four different options for intervention based upon an assessment of both the individual's knowledge and ability to complete the task and willingness or motivation to do so.

Figure 3.1 Four modes of intervention[1]

Guide *Enthusiastic beginner*	**Empower** *Capable and up for the challenge*
Direct *Nervous beginner*	**Excite** *Capable but demotivated*

1 The concept that different people need different styles of intervention was developed by Hersey and Blanchard in their situational leadership theory and this idea was further adapted and enhanced into the skill versus will matrix by Max Landsberg in his book *The Tao of Coaching: Boost your effectiveness at work by inspiring and developing those around you*, first published by HarperCollins in 1996.

Looking in depth at the four quadrants you can see that you need to tailor your approach very significantly if you are to get the best out of people.

Direct – these are people with low levels of skill and experience who are not used to taking on additional responsibility. If you delegate to these people, you should start with relatively straightforward, well-bounded tasks that are likely to recur soon, so that they can get additional practice at the same sort of activity. You will need to:

- tell them what to do and provide a step-by-step guide on how to do it;
- check their understanding;
- provide clear rules and deadlines;
- give them just enough training as they are about to take on the task;
- provide frequent feedback against progress;
- supervise closely – praise and nurture.

Guide – these people are ready and eager for the challenge, but don't have the skills and knowledge required to perform well. They probably don't realise how little they know and, in their eagerness, are likely to charge into things and often make mistakes: mistakes that they may not recognise. They still need lots of direction, but you will need to be subtle about how you do it as they tend to be impatient:

- Explain what you need them to do and suggest in broad terms how they may go about it. Suggest they bring back a detailed plan of action before they start work.
- Check their plan and confirm their understanding of what outcomes need to be produced.
- Check their understanding by asking them to think through what might go wrong and where they may need help.

- Identify people they can talk to who have done something similar.

- Monitor, provide feedback and praise.

- Control without demotivating, and relax the frequency and depth of your controls as progress is made.

Excite – these people are well able to do the required task, but are reluctant to step up to the plate. They may have had a previous bad experience or may not have learned to trust you. Managers often ignore, or sideline, this sort of person as being too difficult. These are key resources and need to be engaged for their benefit and the benefit of the team. You will need to:

- Explain what needs to be achieved and why they are well suited to the task.

- Spend time with them to identify the reasons for their reluctance. Is it a question of your management style or some previous bad experience or some other personal factors?

- Energise and engage them – use them as a sounding board for ideas, show that you value their input, and include them in scoping the task and defining the outputs and quality criteria to be used.

- Develop a coaching relationship with the objective of their personal growth. Remember that the relationship between coach and coachee must be elective and trust based. You may be their manager, but you may not be the best person to coach them.

- Monitor and provide frequent feedback and praise.

- Ensure that they get wider recognition for their efforts – involve them in presentations to clients or senior leaders. Sing their praises to the rest of the team.

Empower – these people are ready and eager for the challenge; if you don't harness their energy, they will probably find a way to go around you. These are candidates for your succession planning. You should go beyond just delegating tasks to these people – you need to delegate decision making, as this is a key management skill. With these people you need to:

- Talk about the desired outcomes and ask them how they would achieve them.

- Use analytical and explorative questions to check that they have considered every angle in relation to the problem or opportunity.

- Involve them in decision making and the identification of additional resources.

- Give them responsibility for getting other people up to speed and provide the necessary training.

- Adopt a coaching style in order to grow your 'star performer'.

- Look for opportunities to praise and encourage, don't ignore or over-manage them.

- Celebrate their successes.

THINGS FOR YOU TO WORK ON NOW

Delegation must be a purposeful activity done in a thoughtful way. Don't wait for a crisis, an emergency or a deadline to prompt you to delegate activities; in such circumstances you will not be in the right state of mind to delegate effectively.

Below are some questions to ask yourself to help you adopt a more structured approach to delegation that benefits your staff and helps you at the same time.

KEY QUESTIONS TO ASK YOURSELF

- If I had an extra day per week, what could I do with it that would produce long-term benefit for the company and me?

- If I had one day fewer per week, what tasks could I give up, or give to someone else, without degrading the overall performance of my department?

- If I had to nominate one of my team to step into my job, who would I choose and why?

- What are the three or four key characteristics and behaviours that I need to see in a team member before I can start to trust and rely on them?

- What have I done recently to make sure that all my team members understand those three or four characteristics that I really value?

The above questions will give you some insight into who you need to develop and what you need to focus upon. Below are some practical tools that can help you plan your approach and monitor your own progress.

MINI EXERCISES YOU CAN TRY IMMEDIATELY

- Carry out a personal audit of how you have spent your time over the past two weeks. Now focus in on the actual time you spent doing tasks that produce outputs that are needed by internal or external customers. Score each of these tasks using a 1 to 5 scale, where 5 means only you could possibly do it and 1 means pretty much anyone in your team could have done it. All the tasks that scored 3 or below are strong candidates for delegation and you should make a personal commitment to find a way of delegating these tasks.

- Look at the time you spent developing members of your team – make a commitment to double the time you devote to these activities over the next two weeks and monitor how your team respond to this new approach.

- Identify two members of your team to whom you can start to delegate tasks. After two weeks, add another team member into the mix of people you are growing – make sure that over the next three months you spend time developing each and every member of your team. Make a new personal rule – no favourites.

FURTHER FOOD FOR THE CURIOUS

Harvard Business Essentials (2005) Delegation: Gaining time for yourself. In: *Time Management: Increase your personal productivity and effectiveness*. Boston: Harvard Business School Press. 63–76:

- This is a good primer that links the related arts of delegation and time management, and provides practical tips and advice.

Keller Johnson L. (2007) Are You Delegating So it Sticks? *Harvard Business Review*, September. Available from https://hbr.org/product/update-classic-are-you-delegating-so-it-sticks/U0709B-PDF-ENG [21 March 2017]:

- This short paper sets out five big ideas to help you become more effective in delegation.

4 DEALING WITH POOR PERFORMANCE

The focus of this chapter is developing the leader's ability to help their staff achieve and sustain peak performance. Performance management is not an annual event, it is an ongoing process that needs the leader's attention every hour of every day; putting off difficult conversations only makes things even more difficult in the long run.

WHY IS THIS IMPORTANT?

In the modern world organisations continually expect you to do more with less. The pressure to produce and deliver is probably greater today than ever before and, if certain individuals are not pulling their weight, then those that do so are under even greater pressure.

Poor performers inject most of the mistakes and errors into a task, which usually has a knock-on effect down the line, resulting in rework and fire-fighting. Rework adds significantly to the cost base but what really kills a project is undiscovered rework. Costs rise rapidly as the time lapse between making a mistake and discovering it increases.

In addition, poor performers can invade an organisation like a virus; most managers have little experience or appetite for dealing with poor performance so rather than have a difficult conversation it is often easier to find a way of moving the problem elsewhere; consequently, poor performers can get passed around from pillar to post as each leader, in turn, tries to rid themselves of the problem. This lack of willingness to grasp the nettle combined with a reluctance to say or write critical comments in an appraisal often leads to poor performers having a history of appraisals that, whilst not glowing, do not accurately reflect the true performance. When successive managers fail to address the poor performance issue and duck the problem, it becomes very difficult, if not impossible, to take the person through formal disciplinary procedures when they do eventually get a leader with the courage to do so.

THE IMPACT OF THE ISSUE

In virtually every organisation, people are your biggest budget item and, if you are honest, you could probably point the finger at certain individuals who you do not perceive to be 'pulling their weight'. If people are not performing there is often a triggering event or set of circumstances that created or contributed to the offending behaviour. If you can uncover and remove the source of the irritation the behaviour may miraculously improve. Sometimes you may find that your leadership style is part of the problem.

MOST PEOPLE RESPOND TO STROKING

Paul, a team leader, was having issues with his deputy. His deputy seemed to be incapable of keeping meetings on track and sticking to an agenda; in addition he was upsetting other members of the team. Paul would have corrective conversations with his deputy but after a few days his deputy would slip back into his old ways. Paul asked a colleague for advice and discovered that he, Paul, was part of the problem. Paul was pointing out his deputy's mistakes but failing to praise and therefore encourage and reinforce positive behaviour. When he started praising, encouraging and supporting as opposed to criticising, his deputy's behaviour changed for the better.

Dealing with poor performance is difficult, time-consuming and fraught with danger; hence it is often avoided. For many organisations, in particular the more traditional and longer-standing ones, dealing with poor performance is one of the principal 'zones of uncomfortable debate', that is, a key issue that needs to be addressed, that is holding the organisation back, but which is just too uncomfortable to talk about.

MAKING SENSE OF IT ALL

There are two key aspects that contribute towards one's performance: capability and attitude. When we talk about capability, we are considering the holistic combination of a person's knowledge, skills and experience. When we talk about attitude, we are considering their willingness to contribute, to collaborate and to learn – all of which should be done with a positive intent for the greater good.

When dealing with poor performance, it is important to distinguish between temporary glitches and long-term degradation. The former needs to be nipped in the bud swiftly and simply by following the steps you will find at the beginning of the practical advice section.

In the case of long-term degradation in performance, it is important to understand the root causes and to work with the person to reverse the trend. The model in Figure 4.1 will help you to make sense of a situation and identify the root cause.

Problem children – these people are your biggest challenge; they have neither the capability nor the right attitude. They could be young, insecure and just starting out, they could be approaching retirement and marking time, or they may have been left in the wrong job for too long and become disillusioned. Whatever the reason, they will need coaching, counselling and motivating in order to move them to a better place.

Figure 4.1 Performance portfolio

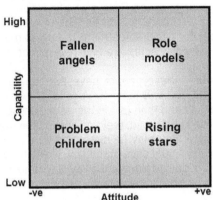

PLAY TO STRENGTHS NOT WEAKNESSES

The manager of a small team of database analysts (DBAs) had one member that was a 'problem child'. She could deal with the simple tasks but anything that was difficult or complicated seemed to be beyond her intellectual capability. The manager, with her agreement, redefined her role playing to her strengths whilst at the same time relieving the other team members of tasks which they found boring. She became a 'role model' in her new capacity.

Rising stars – these are your people with the right attitude, but without the necessary capability. They may be youngsters just starting out, members of your team who have just taken on a new role, or possibly people who have been promoted too soon. Training and development may be the answer in the case of the former. In the case of the latter, you may need to consider adjustment to their role or even changing it for a more suitable one. Either way, employees in this category need to be nurtured and protected. It is important to recognise that whenever someone takes on a new role, they will, by definition, be lacking capability, so the key issue is how quickly they can adjust and get up to speed. People who find themselves on the management fast-track tend to be those who demonstrate a clear capacity for rapid adjustment to new demands and an ability to very quickly achieve a high level of competence.

Fallen angels – these people have the capability, but the wrong attitude. You will need to uncover the reason for the negative attitude and then tackle the issue head on. They may be underutilised and bored, they may be in the wrong job and, hence, unhappy, they may be distracted by a personal issue or just plain lazy. In the case of the last, virtually everyone can be motivated to do something; the key is finding out what that something is.

BEING BORED IS NOT THE SAME AS BEING INCOMPETENT

An analyst programmer had become a 'fallen angel'. Her manager had a hunch and took a risk and made her up to team leader. She responded very positively to her new role, enjoyed the challenge and became a 'role model'. The problem had been boredom and frustration in a role that did not stretch her.

Role models – these people are your top performers; the challenge here is to ensure they remain so. In order to achieve this, they will need to be cherished and rewarded. If you let complacency set in and just expect them to get on with it, they will either get demotivated or leave. Role models need to be stretched and challenged; initially this will be by giving them greater exposure to decision making, cross-functional activities and forward planning. As they grow further, you will need to find opportunities for them to leave you, but grow in the wider business. You must, therefore, accept that people in the role-model sector will, and indeed must, leave you and that your job is to make sure that when they move on, they do so within the company and they do so for a more challenging job.

EVEN GOOD PEOPLE GO WRONG

Tom, a 'role model', became a 'fallen angel' when he inherited a new boss who he didn't respect. Tom felt micro-managed and believed that his strengths and talents were unrecognised. After a short period of time, during which Tom nearly left his organisation, Tom rose to the challenge; he took the initiative to coach his boss to become a better boss.

In the next section, we will give practical advice on how to deal with the four different types of performance.

PRACTICAL ADVICE

Before you can start to deal with any performance issue, there are a few questions you need to ask yourself, and a few things that you need to ensure are in place:

- Have you clearly communicated what is expected in terms of outcome, that is, what needs to be achieved, when it needs to be achieved and how success will be measured?

- Does the person have the appropriate skills, or have they undergone the necessary training to enable them to complete the task?

- Do they have access to the information and resources they need?

- Challenge your own leadership ability; could part of the problem lie at your doorstep?

  - Have you delegated with sufficient clarity?

  - Have you been there to provide support and guidance when needed?

- Have you adequately prioritised, so that they understand what is important and why?

- Is this a real issue and not one of a personality clash or difference in style?

- Do you have the real-time evidence to support your claim of poor performance? You must ensure that you are not relying upon hearsay.

- Do they have a personal issue that is affecting their performance?

Having satisfied the above, you need to tackle the issue in a timely manner, that is, shortly after it occurs. Don't wait for appraisal time – that is far, far too late. You should immediately take the following steps in this order:

- Tell them very clearly that their performance is not of an acceptable standard. Never criticise them as a person, only their behaviour.

- Give them the opportunity to explain why their performance was not up to standard. If, for example, something dreadful had happened to a family member the previous day, you would feel very foolish if you had just laid into them for not performing at their best.

- Be very clear about why the performance is substandard and the impact of their performance on others and the wider context of the organisation as a whole.

- Say how you feel about the situation.

- State, explicitly, what is at stake.

- If appropriate, be honest about your own part in creating the issue.

- Give them the opportunity to explain the situation from their point of view. Keep quiet and actively listen to what they have to say.

- Confirm a common understanding of the issue and then agree a sequence of steps necessary to rectify the situation.

- Agree any follow-up actions that you, the manager, need to take.

- Make sure that they have a workable plan for what they need to do and agree when and how you will check on their progress. Thank them for their input.

- Keep clear records to aid follow-up activities and support future conversations.

- Keep on top of the situation – do not expect a quick fix, but also do not let it slip off your priority list.

Now we will move on to consider how best to deal with the issue of long-term degradation in performance. You will need to use a feedback and developmental approach appropriate to the person's capability and attitude, and we will use the model outlined in the previous section to structure our advice.

Dealing with your problem children – the first step is to find out what the problem is with your problem child. Are they a nervous starter or long-serving cynic? Have they been over-promoted or ended up in a role that bores them to tears? Once you have identified the root cause, you will need to determine the most appropriate corrective action. This may include any one or a number of the following:

- Training – would the person benefit from either skill-based training or behavioural training?

- Coaching – would this person benefit from being asked some probing questions to challenge their thinking and behaviour, in particular some reflective questions to get them thinking about why they did what they did? You should also encourage them to honestly examine the motives that underpinned their actions. Finally, you need to help them think through the impact that their poor performance is having on others.

- Mentoring – are they lacking in self-confidence and in need of reassurance or affirmation from someone with greater experience?

- Motivation – could you enhance their role in any way to make it more appealing?

- Counselling – do they need professional help to resolve a personal issue?

- Consider a change in job role – are they in the right job? Have they been over-promoted, and are they struggling with both the task and their emotions as a consequence?

- If none of the above strategies achieve the desired result, you may need to take people through formal disciplinary procedures. Ensure that you follow the formal process, as laid down by your human resources (HR) department, starting with an informal verbal warning and progressing, if need be, to formal written warnings.

- As a last resort, you might need to consider managing them out of the organisation or towards early retirement. Here is where you may benefit from the assistance of your HR department and outplacement organisations.

Dealing with your rising stars – the first step is to understand their potential. Are they bright, able and quick to learn or do they get there through tenacity and hard work? Once you have established their potential and what interests and motivates them, you will be able to agree an appropriate developmental plan. Your prime tools will include:

- Training – this may be skill-based or behavioural training.

- Coaching – would this person benefit from being asked some probing questions to clarify their understanding of what is expected of them and how confident they feel in achieving it, some explorative questions to open their mind to new possibilities, or some fresh questions to challenge their basic thinking and 'eternal truths'?

- Mentoring – would this person benefit from mirroring someone with greater experience or guidance in their judgement of situations and their consequential decision making?

Dealing with your fallen angels – the first step is to uncover the root cause of the bad attitude. Is it because they are bored, unhappy, disgruntled, feeling bullied or just plain lazy? Have they been ignored, forgotten about or ended up in the wrong job? You may wish to consider:

- Coaching – would this person benefit from being asked some probing questions to invite more detail in relation to their attitude problem, some reflective questions to get them thinking about why they behave the way they do and to examine their motives, some affective questions to consider the impact their attitude is having on others, or some explorative questions to open their mind to new perspectives?

- Mentoring – could the issue be one of lack of self-confidence? If so, they may be in need of affirmation or guidance from someone with greater experience than themselves.

- Counselling – do they need professional help to resolve a personal issue?

- Do they feel bullied? – if so, the problem may well lie at your doorstep.

- Job enrichment – could you enhance or supplement their role to make it more fulfilling/appealing?

- Consider a change in job role – do they need greater responsibility or a new challenge?

The final quadrant of the model deals with people you have classified as role models. You would not expect to have performance issues with these people, but that does not mean that you can afford to ignore them. With these people, your focus should be on maintaining and sustaining actions and providing intellectual and professional challenges.

Ensuring your role models remain just that – such valuable members of your team will need to be cherished, nurtured and rewarded. If you don't do this, they will either leave, or become fallen angels. Focus on the following actions:

- Provide opportunities for personal development and help prepare them for the next step up.

- Give them frequent and positive feedback – ensure that they know that they are doing a good job, and that they know how much you value and appreciate them.

- Coach them – specifically in areas where they will need to exercise judgement and decision making. Stretch them and encourage them to aim for higher goals; challenge them to think the unthinkable and to generate new insights.

- Reward their achievements and celebrate their successes.

- Give them opportunities to represent you in discussions with other departments and other businesses.

- Help them to develop their circle of influence, and to develop wider knowledge of the business and its operating environment.

- Involve them in discussions about strategic direction and planning the development of junior colleagues.

- Identify opportunities for them to act as coaches for junior colleagues.

- Could you enhance their job in any way to increase their job satisfaction?

Any discussions about performance issues will be emotionally charged. Therefore, it is imperative that you remember the importance of tone, body language and facial expression. Make use of silence to help both of you to get in touch with what you really want to say, and ensure there is space for reflection and active listening. Ensure at all times that you engage in a genuine two-way conversation, rather than letting your discussions deteriorate into a one-way monologue.

Get to know your staff; understand both their hearts and their minds. Ensure the dialogue is ongoing. Use active questioning to establish what excites and what frustrates them. Actively listen to the nuances and subtext to get beneath the surface.

Develop a strong interest in motivational psychology. Be prepared to accept short-term pain for long-term gain. Your reward will be motivated, energised and loyal staff.

The Golden Rule is that performance management is not a once a year activity that coincides with the annual appraisal.

Every day is an opportunity to manage performance.

THINGS FOR YOU TO WORK ON NOW

Before you start to work with anyone on any aspect of performance you need to understand the context in which the performance is deemed to be lacking and you need to be fully aware of the historical path that led this individual into their current place. Take a few moments to quietly think about the following questions. Build these types of reflective questions into your own personal planning and do it on a regular basis.

KEY QUESTIONS TO ASK YOURSELF

- Am I concerned about the performance of any member of my team? The answer is probably yes, otherwise you would not be reading this chapter.

- If so, how have I dealt with the situation in the past? What is my approach towards dealing with poor performance?

- If you do have poor performers, how has this been handled within the appraisal process and formal HR procedures?

- What is the general attitude and approach towards poor performance in my company?

- Honestly consider if you, yourself, could be part of the problem.

Now use the tools we have discussed to start to plan how you will manage the performance of your team differently. When you do the attitude versus capability assessment on your team it is best to do it at home and keep all your notes there.

MINI EXERCISES YOU CAN TRY IMMEDIATELY

- Use the attitude versus capability matrix to analyse the performance of your team. Classify each member of your team and plot them on the matrix. How many do you have in each category? (Your analysis is for your eyes only – keep it safe from prying eyes.)

- Draw up and agree a plan for dealing with one of your 'fallen angels'. Analyse the experience – what went well and what didn't go so well? Now refine your approach and repeat with another of your fallen angels.

- Draw up and agree a plan for dealing with one of your 'rising stars'. Analyse the experience – what went well and what didn't go so well? Now refine your approach and repeat with another of your rising stars.

- Having learned from these two groups, you are now ready to tackle your 'problem children'.

FURTHER FOOD FOR THE CURIOUS

Scott S. (2002) *Fierce Conversations: Achieving success at work and in life, one conversation at a time.* New York: The Penguin Group:

- An enlightening and practical book on achieving results through skilful and courageous dialogue.

5   BEHAVING WITH A TRUE SENSE OF URGENCY

This chapter will help you cut through the noise and bustle of your daily grind and identify those things that really matter. The most effective employees are those who know how to focus their action and attention on those things that directly contribute to desired outcomes. As a leader, you need to develop the ability to focus and you need to inculcate that same ability in all of your staff.

WHY IS THIS IMPORTANT?

Nowadays people live in a world where they can have pretty much instant access to anything they want 24 hours a day, seven days a week. Our society seems to crave instant gratification; people want success and they want it now. Against this background and an ever-increasing pace of life, it is easy to believe that when you respond very quickly, you are behaving with urgency and that to strive for an even quicker speed of reaction is the right thing to do. The reality is that urgency and speed of reaction **are not** the same thing. Urgency is not about speed; it is about focus and energy – focusing relentlessly on what is important for survival, for growth and for change and to do it now, not sometime in the future when you have time in your busy schedule.

Most managers believe that they have created urgency when they see lots of people running around doing lots of things. Paradoxically, in order to have the time to behave with urgency, it is often necessary to do less – that is, to create the space needed to think about the future, to be able to take action when action is needed, to make commitments and follow them through. At a time when you seem to be constantly running faster just to stay in the same place, when your diaries are crowded with back-to-back meetings from 8.00 a.m. to 7.00 p.m., clearing the space to be able to devote time to take focused, important and energetic action may appear to be an impossible task, but it is essential and you must find a way to achieve it.

THE IMPACT OF THE ISSUE

Leaders are not paid to do the routine tasks that keep the wheels turning; that is the role of team leaders and supervisors. Most day-to-day operations can take care of themselves without much attention, or oversight, from the leader. What the leader is paid to do is to find new and novel ways to make the wheels go around more effectively.

Better still, they are there to envisage and create an organisation that doesn't run on wheels, but rather has some sort of frictionless super-drive that costs less to run and produces more output with greater quality and customer satisfaction.

In short, leaders are paid to achieve the extraordinary, rather than the ordinary.

REFRAMING A PROBLEM TO GAIN A SENSE OF URGENCY

For many months, a CIO had been struggling to get his peers to make a decision on IT security. They didn't get his high-level pitch and switched off when he went into the detail. A new development manager suggested an alternative strategy and sketched a Maslow-type hierarchy of needs relating to security in one's own home as illustrated below.

Figure 5.1 Using an analogy to reframe a problem

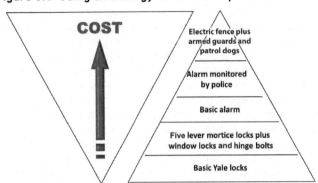

He then asked the security team to provide an estimated cost at each level of the model for an equivalent level of security for the business. The Board was impressed. Framing the question in this way facilitated a decision within 30 minutes. The CIO had enhanced his standing within the organisation and the new development manager had enhanced his reputation in the eyes of his CIO.

You cannot achieve extraordinary things when you are bogged down with other people's trivia and noise, which they should be dealing with themselves. Many leaders either feel that they are powerless to achieve anything other than maintain the status quo, or they feel afraid to try anything different in case it fails; sometimes they may really have the desire, but they just cannot find the time, or the energy, because they are so busy doing the less important stuff. It is also important to remember that as a leader you are also a role model for your team; if they see you running around like a headless chicken they are likely to adopt the same behaviour. You need to focus on the important tasks and you need your team to understand what is important and focus their attentions accordingly.

MAKING SENSE OF IT ALL

A sense of urgency is not to be confused with frantic activity focused on meeting upon meeting, fire-fighting, back protecting or the pursuit of the trivial or the unimportant. Urgency is about focusing on a few key things and then making the time and finding the energy to see those key things through to completion. In their article 'Beware the busy manager', Bruch and Ghoshal report on their findings from 10 years spent studying senior managers in organisations around the world. They suggest that, in their experience, as many as 90 per cent of all managers squander their time on all sorts of ineffective activity. They call it 'active non-action', a great expression that neatly describes the sort of frantic posturing that we see from many managers. The big question is what do you have to do to be a part of the 10 per cent of managers who are apparently focused enough to make a difference?

Bruch and Ghoshal identify four types of behaviour associated with how a manager approaches their job: the disengaged, the procrastinator, the distracted and the purposeful. We will look specifically at the purposeful manager, as that is the model to which you should aspire.

Perhaps the thing that most distinguishes the purposeful manager is the way they define themselves with respect to their work and their autonomy for action. Many IT leaders appear to be content to sit in a box defined by others — by their peers, their job description, the business environment and what other people think will work or is appropriate. They operate only within the confines of how their box has been defined.

Purposeful managers are not constrained by the hand that life deals them — they don't play the cards, even when they know they hold a losing hand. What they do is trade in the cards to get a better hand. They use their network to access required resources, they cultivate relationships with influential people, and they build and acquire competencies with the sole aim of increasing their freedom to act. The most important word in this paragraph is 'purposeful': we are not suggesting that you become embroiled in political posturing – we are suggesting that you make yourself and your team aware of the key outcomes that you need to achieve and that you and your team become single minded in doing whatever is necessary to ensure that the desired outcomes are achieved.

THE BANKING DIRECTOR'S REQUEST

A team leader within a financial services company received a request from the banking director that was neither practical nor feasible. Instead of saying 'no' or giving a prohibitive estimate, the team leader used questioning techniques to ascertain the business driver behind the request. This led the team leader to suggest an alternative, cloud-based solution that was relatively simple and inexpensive to implement. The bank trialled the idea over a three-month period and monitored the volumes and type of activity. Armed with this information, the banking director made a somewhat different, but wiser, business decision than was previously possible. IT had truly exceeded expectations and delighted their business partner.

So, acting with urgency and purpose is about proactively managing your environment to increase your choice and freedom to act, and then acting with focus on one or two key initiatives to the exclusion of all else, and maintaining energy throughout until your goal is achieved.

THE OFFICE MOVE

Tom, a newly appointed project manager, was given responsibility for project managing an office move in a bank's expanding Parisian subsidiary. The physical move was to take place over a bank holiday weekend. All went according to plan apart from the non-arrival, via courier from the UK, of some small, but vital, hardware components. It was 5.00 p.m. on the Saturday and Tom phoned around all the computer stores until he had located what he needed. He offered the store an extra 100 euros if they would stay open until 6.00 p.m.; he then offered the taxi driver double his fare if he could get him there within half-an-hour. Tom's quick thinking and novel actions had saved the day!

PRACTICAL ADVICE

We have suggested that the purposeful manager is one who understands the value of focus and applied energy, and also appreciates that these are the two qualities that technology and the modern organisational structure appear to be set up to steal from you. As such, the first rule of acting with urgency and purpose is to actively manage your time – if you allow yourself to be swept along at the pace of others you will lose focus and deplete your reserves of energy.

Here are some basic rules for you to adopt, and we strongly recommend that once you feel the benefit that this brings, you should encourage your team to adopt the same values and practices:

- Set aside specific times of day to deal with email, phone calls and visitors. The most purposeful managers are rigorous about protecting their time:

  - Turn off all alerts on your phone and PC – you are not its servant; it is yours. If you start to respond to everything as it hits you, there is no way that you can prioritise.

  - Assess the importance of a task in relation to your 'purpose'. Your prime measure should be 'does this task contribute to the one or two primary initiatives that I have set myself, or accepted from the leadership team?'

- Increasingly, leaders don't have personal assistants to protect them and they have open electronic diaries that everyone can see. This may be very egalitarian and the modern equivalent of saying 'my door is always open', but it is certainly a sure-fire way of letting other people fill your day with stuff that is important to them, but may be irrelevant to you. Get into the habit of blocking out at least 40 per cent of your time each week – use software functionality to show the time as busy and private. Make a rule that the only people who can steal this time from you are people well above your own pay grade.

- Build in time to reflect on what is happening and what your priorities are. For instance, if you have a one-hour commute to work by car, it may be an idea to designate the morning commute as your reflection time and have your mobile phone turned off. The evening commute, by contrast, may become known to your staff as the time to run things past you or to give you catch-up status reports. Encourage them to talk to you rather than email you. If you need an audit trail, you can always ask them for a short confirmation email. As well as creating time to focus, you also need to find ways of reducing stress and topping up your energy levels. This is an individual and personal need that is likely to be fulfilled outside the work environment by:

  - engaging in an absorbing hobby;

  - doing sport, exercise or meditation;

  - giving something back to your local community – strangely, sometimes the more energy you expend, the more you seem to have.

Once you have got hold of your time and you have found the wellsprings of energy you need for the journey, you must focus all your attention on the journey itself. This requires you to address a meaningful challenge, something that is bigger than your immediate department. It should be of importance to the continued growth and sustainability of your organisation; you should have choice in the way you approach the challenge and you need to enlist the support of your network to gain broad organisational acceptance that finding a solution to this challenge or opportunity will produce lasting value for the organisation.

Once you have found such a challenge, it is easy to see what needs to be focused upon and how you will recognise when you have been successful. It has to be something that you are prepared to make a very visible personal commitment to and also something that you are prepared to bet your reputation on. If your challenge is meaningful and relevant you will find that, as you talk about it with colleagues and staff, people will spontaneously volunteer to come on the journey with you – a real acid test of the organisational value of an initiative is its ability to spontaneously engage and inspire others.

Without such a challenge, urgency can only be maintained for very short periods. It is the difference between the 200-metre sprint and the marathon. Behaving with a sense of urgency is about the long game and finding the reserves of energy and commitment that can carry you through the 26 miles of the marathon to the finishing line.

THINGS FOR YOU TO WORK ON NOW

You have seen that urgency is about focus and focus can only be sustained if it is directly connected to some deeper sense of purpose. You need to find and tap into your deep sense of purpose, you need to know how that purpose brings into focus the key initiatives that your team is tasked to deliver against and then you need to help the members of your team find their own share in that purpose. You cannot give others a sense of purpose but you can help them find a way to share in and contribute towards a common purpose. Often in the daily grind of getting things done and reacting to other people's crises it is easy to lose connection with your sense of purpose. Think quietly and deeply about the questions listed below, try to find in yourself something that is meaningful and is consistent with your value structure. If all else fails at least try to find your share of a wider purpose.

KEY QUESTIONS TO ASK YOURSELF

- What is important to me – how do I want to make a contribution to this organisation and why am I uniquely placed to make that contribution?

- What does the organisation need to achieve in order to survive and prosper? What is my part in this journey?

- What have I done this week to increase my circle of influence and thus gain more support and freedom of action?

- What do I need to concentrate on in the next three months in order to increase my influence and freedom of action even further?

Once you have discovered a sense of purpose you need to set about creating the space and the focus to give that purpose the attention it deserves. The techniques listed below will help you see where and how you can create some space.

MINI EXERCISES YOU CAN TRY IMMEDIATELY

- Do an audit of your diary for the past two weeks – how much of your time was focused on bringing about something new for your organisation? Don't count talking-shops or project-update meetings – we are interested in tangible actions that you took that could bring something new to fruition.

- Look at your diary for the next two weeks – purge the time bandits, get rid of the stuff that just spins wheels. Block out some 'me' time so that you can reflect upon why you are a leader and what you are going to achieve that is unique and different in the next 12 months.

FURTHER FOOD FOR THE CURIOUS

Bruch H. and Ghoshal S. (2002) Beware the Busy Manager. *Harvard Business Review*, February. Available from https://hbr.org/2002/02/beware-the-busy-manager [21 March 2017]:

- This is an insightful article that opens the box on what managers really do and how they fritter away their time. The stunning conclusion is that fully 90 per cent of managers squander their time on ineffective activities. The good news is that the paper identifies the characteristics of different management behaviours and provides useful pointers on how to become more purposeful.

Kotter J.P. (2008) *A Sense of Urgency*. Boston: Harvard Business Press:

- This short and engaging book provides an explanation of the tactics that have been found to be effective in creating urgency during change initiatives.

INDEX

relationship-building exercise 5

respect 1, 2, 7, 10, 20, 41

responsibility 5, 28, 31, 33, 45

rewarding achievements 40, 45, 46

rework 36

rising stars 39–40, 44, 48

role models 39, 40, 41, 45–6

sense of humour 20

Skype 16

small talk 15, 16, 18

social networking 11

speaking well of others 19

specialist groups 18

stress 4, 24, 26, 27, 55

stroking 37

taking an interest in others 19

The 7 Habits of Highly Effective People 12–13

'The Human Moment at Work' 16

time bandits 57

training 6, 31, 33, 39, 41, 43, 44

trust
  delegation 32, 34; increasing organisational influence 10–11, 12, 13–15, 17, 20, 21, 22–3; value of leadership role 2–3, 6, 7

under-acknowledged staff 18–19

urgency, sense of
  energy 49, 50, 51, 52, 53–4, 55–6; focus 49, 50, 51–3, 54, 55–6, 57;

importance of 49–50; key questions 57; mini exercises 57; practical advice 54–6; purposeful managers 52–7; reframing problems 50–1

value of leadership role
  developing professional leadership persona 6–7; dos and don'ts of team leadership 5–6; helping a team member 3; importance of 1–2; key questions 7; mini exercises 8; organisational access 3–4; practical advice 4–6; respect of team members 1, 2; trust 2–3, 6, 7

video-conferencing 16